WARRIOR PRINCESS

CROWNED FOR PURPOSE

WORKBOOK

ANN MARIE COOPER

Warrior Princess: Crowned for Purpose
Copyright 2025 by Ann Marie Cooper. All rights reserved.

Unless otherwise indicated, all Scripture quotations are taken from the Holy Bible, New
International Version® (NIV®). Copyright © 1973, 1978, 1984, 2011 by Biblica, Inc.™
Used by permission. All rights reserved worldwide.

Published in the United States of America

First Printing, 2025

ISBN-13: 978-1-952833-67-0
ISBN-10: 1-952833-67-1

Cover design by TJS Publishing House

Photography by Ideal Moment Photography
1661 Walkup Ave Suite H
Monroe, NC 28110
(980) 327-6681
Idealmomentphotography.com

Publishing assistance provided by TJS Publishing House
PO BOX 25058
Charlotte, NC 2229
www.tjspublishinghouse.com
contact@tjspublishinghouse.com

DEDICATION

To My Daughter Jayden Lynn, You are my inspiration. My Warrior Princess. Your courage, wisdom, compassion, and strength have shaped me in ways I never expected.

Because of you, I discovered my identity and purpose in life.

After your birth, I experienced the profound goodness of God in a way I never had before. Then came the moment, much like Abraham placing Isaac on the altar, when God asked me to surrender you to His will and trust that He had your best interests at heart.

It wasn't easy, but it was so worth it.

In that surrender, I found my God-given purpose.

"But blessed is the one who trusts in the Lord, whose confidence is in him. They will be like a tree planted by the water that sends out its roots by the stream. It does not fear when heat comes; its leaves are always green. It has no worries in a year of drought and never fails to bear fruit."

~ Jeremiah 17:7-8

ACKNOWLEDGMENTS

To my Heavenly Father, this book belongs to You. Every word reflects Your grace, healing, and unshakable purpose for my life. Thank You for calling me, sustaining me, and crowning me with a mission far beyond anything I could have imagined. May *Warrior Princess: Crowned for Purpose* lead many daughters back to Your heart.

To my parents, thank you for laying the foundation of faith in my life. Your love, prayers, and example have shaped me into the woman and warrior I am today. I honor you.

To TJS Publishing House, thank you for believing in this vision and bringing it to life with such excellence. Your guidance made this dream tangible, and I'm so grateful for your dedication to amplifying messages that matter.

To All For One Church, thank you for being a place of community, covering, and kingdom vision. Your support has been a springboard for this calling, and your faith in action has inspired my own.

To the TRUE Trauma Healing board and founding sponsors, thank you for championing the mission before the world could see it. You've helped birth something eternal.

To every woman who's walked with me, prayed with me, and believed in this calling, you are part of the crown. Your stories, encouragement, and faithfulness have been priceless gifts.

To my retreat sisters, you are the heartbeat of this movement. Your bravery to confront your past, embrace your identity, and rise with purpose is what made this book possible.

And to all readers, consider this book your invitation to rise. Out of brokenness comes beauty. Out of injustice, a calling. Out of remembrance, a mission. You are a Warrior Princess, Crowned for Purpose.

INTRODUCTION

Welcome, Warrior Princess.

You're holding more than a book; you're holding a calling.
This devotional workbook was born from a personal journey through
brokenness, healing, and divine purpose. It was written for women like you:
strong, tender-hearted, courageous, and called. Whether you feel like you're in
the middle of a battle or standing at the edge of a breakthrough, this is your
invitation to rise and remember who you are in Christ.

Within these pages, you'll walk through five gemstone virtues:

Courage (Ruby)
Wisdom (Sapphire)
Faith (Amethyst)
Strength (Emerald)
Compassion (Rose Quartz)

Each session blends scripture, personal reflection, and a story of a woman, both
biblical and historical, who lived out her God-given identity with purpose. In
Pocahontas' story, you'll see a familiar thread of boldness, surrender, and legacy.
Her story isn't meant for fairy-tale inspiration, but to reflect something many of
us understand: pain, sacrifice, and destiny.

As you read, you'll find places where I pour out my heart. You'll see the
wrestling and the redemption, the waiting and rising, the pain and the power.
I've walked this road, and now I walk it with you.

This isn't just a workbook. It's a mirror to reflect who you truly are: a daughter
of the King, a Warrior Princess, crowned with purpose.
So, open your heart. Ask God to meet you in each moment. He will.
Because this is your time to rise, Warrior Princess.
And the crown you've been longing for?
It's already yours.

With love and expectation,

Ann Marie Cooper, *Founder*
TRUE Trauma Healing

CONTENTS

How to Use This Devotional

First and foremost, use this workbook to get to know the One who created you.

Get to know His heart, because it is set on your best.

Let the stories of the women in these pages inspire you to become all that you were created to be.

Don't rush. Take your time. Dig deep. Do the work.

You are worth it.

You deserve to know the depth of God's love for you.

"so that Christ may dwell in your hearts through faith. And I pray that you, being rooted and established in love, may have power, together with all the Lord's holy people, to grasp how wide and long and high and deep is the love of Christ, and to know this love that surpasses knowledge - that you may be filled to the measure of all the fullness of God."

Ephesians 3:17–19

Warrior Princess: Crowned for Purpose is more than a book. It's a journey of healing, identity, and calling. Whether you're walking through it on your own, with a small group, or as part of a retreat, this devotional was designed to help you grow in both warrior strength and princess grace, one gem at a time.

Personal Use (Daily or Weekly)

- Start with Prayer: Invite the Holy Spirit to lead your heart as you read.

- Read the Gemstone Theme: Each chapter focuses on one core virtue symbolized by a gem: Courage, Wisdom, Faith, Strength, or

Compassion.

- Engage the Story: Read the personal testimony, biblical example, and Pocahontas parallel to see how God moves through real lives and real battles.

- Go Deeper with Scripture: Use the study prompts to dig into God's Word and reflect on what He's saying to you.

- Armor Up: Read the Warrior Princess Daily Armor devotional at the end of the session and apply it to your week.

- Live the Lesson: Act on what you've learned and place the matching gemstone sticker (or color the gem space) on your tiara.

- Declare the Truth: Speak the matching "I Am" affirmation throughout your day to anchor your identity in Christ.

Group or Bible Study Use

- Open with Worship or Prayer.

- Read the Devotional Together: Take turns reading aloud or follow along silently.

- Discuss the Reflection Questions: Use these to deepen the connection and encourage one another.

- Share Your Stories: Allow space for testimonies, personal breakthroughs, and support.

- End with a Group Declaration: Speak the gemstone's "I Am" statement together for unity and empowerment.

Retreat Experience

- Follow the Schedule: Each gemstone session will be taught live during the retreat.

- Use the Devotional Pages: Journal key takeaways, prayers, and insights after each session.

- Engage in the Activities: Participate in reflection walks, prayer stations, and the Warrior's Crowning Ceremony.

- Place Your Gemstone Sticker: As you complete each session, mark your crown with its gem as a symbol of transformation.

This journey was made for you. As you walk through each page, may you rise with purpose, shine with God's beauty, and live crowned in truth.

You are a Warrior Princess, Crowned for Purpose.

WARRIOR PRINCESS PROFILES:
Women Who Walked in Purpose

Esther
The Hidden Queen with a Bold Purpose
Biblical Figure (Book of Esther)

Courage
Esther was a Jewish orphan raised by her cousin Mordecai and eventually became queen of Persia. Though her beauty gained her favor, it was her bold faith that saved her people. When the Jews faced extermination, Esther risked her life by approaching King Xerxes uninvited. A crime punishable by death. Her famous words still echo: "If I perish, I perish."

Legacy:
• God positions us for purpose, often where we least expect it.
• Courage is often found in obedience, not fearlessness.
• Your voice matters when it's yielded to His call. You were created "For such a time as this..."

Abigail
The Wise Intercessor and Warrior of Peace
Biblical Figure (1 Samuel 25)

Wisdom
Abigail was the intelligent and discerning wife of Nabal, a foolish and harsh man. When David was prepared to destroy her household in anger, Abigail intervened with humility, wisdom, and courage. Her bold act of peacemaking averted bloodshed and won David's respect.

Legacy:
• Discernment is a weapon of the wise.
• Peacemaking often requires courage, not silence.
• Wisdom and humility are marks of spiritual strength

Mary Magdalene

Devoted Witness of Resurrection
Biblical Figure (Gospels)

Faith

Mary Magdalene was healed by Jesus, who cast out seven demons from her (Luke 8:2). After that, she became one of His most faithful followers. She not only supported His ministry but also stood by Him at the cross when others fled. And when He rose from the dead, it was Mary who was the first to see Him and share the good news.

Legacy:
- No past can disqualify a woman set free by Jesus.
- Devotion leads to divine encounters.
- Faithfulness positions you for revelation.

Ruth
The Loyal Redeemed Sojourner
Biblical Figure (Book of Ruth)

Strength

Ruth, a Moabite widow, chose loyalty over comfort. After her husband died, she clung to her mother-in-law Naomi, declaring, "Your people will be my people, and your God my God." Her faith and humility led her to Boaz, her kinsman redeemer, and she became the great-grandmother of King David.

Legacy:
- Faithfulness in the mundane leads to generational impact.
- God writes redemption into the most unlikely stories.
- Loyalty is a powerful form of strength.

The Samaritan Woman
The Redeemed Witness at the Well
Biblical Figure (John 4:1–42)
Compassion:

She came to the well alone at midday, when no one else would be there. This woman had a past. Five husbands. One live-in partner. And a reputation that made her an outcast. But Jesus didn't avoid her. He went out of His way to find her. He revealed her sin, then offered her living water. Transformed by grace, she became one of the first evangelists, telling her village, "Come, see a man who told me everything I ever did!"

Legacy:
• Jesus meets us in our shame and offers redemption.
• No one is too far gone for God's grace.
• Your story becomes your testimony when touched by mercy.

Hannah
The Faithful Intercessor and Mother of Promise
Biblical Figure (1 Samuel 1–2)

Love

Hannah's story begins in quiet anguish. Though deeply loved by her husband, Elkanah, she bore the shame of barrenness. Mocked and misunderstood, she brought her pain to God. She wept, worshiped, and made a vow: "If You give me a son, I will give him back to You." God honored her prayer, and she kept her vow. Samuel's birth became the foundation of prophetic leadership in Israel.

Legacy:
• Waiting is not wasted when it's surrendered to God.
• Prayer opens the door to purpose.
• Honor is born through perseverance and trust.

Pocahontas
The Bridge Between Worlds
Historical Figure (c. 1596–1617)

Pocahontas, the Native American daughter of Chief Powhatan, is remembered for her courage, compassion, and role as a peacemaker during the early colonization of America. She risked her life to intervene and save Captain John Smith and later chose to embrace a new faith and culture when she married John Rolfe, becoming Lady Rebecca Rolfe.

Legacy:

Pocahontas lived at the intersection of two worlds, navigating between her native identity and a new calling that required profound bravery and wisdom. She is a powerful symbol of reconciliation, sacrifice, and transformational identity. Her story echoes the spiritual journey of surrender, bridging the old self and the redeemed life.

Virtue	Warrior Princess Name	Key Scripture
Courage	Esther	Esther 4:14
Wisdom	Abigail	1 Samuel 25:32–33
Faith	Mary Magdalene	Luke 8:2 John 20:16–18
Strength	Ruth	Ruth 1:16–17
Compassion	Samaritan Woman	John 4:28–30, 39
Love	Hannah	1 Samuel 1:10–11, 27–28
Cultural Parallel	Pocahontas	Proverbs 3:5–6

On this journey, you will meet a historical figure who left a deep impact on my faith journey: Pocahontas.

From a young age, Pocahontas captured my heart, not just as a character, but as a real woman of courage and compassion. Born into royalty, she lived as a servant-leader and a bridge between worlds. After being taken as ransom in a time of conflict, she was treated with kindness, introduced to the teachings of Jesus, and embraced Christianity. She was later baptized as Rebecca, taking on a new name and a new identity in faith.

To me, she represents the heart of this journey: a woman who laid down comfort for calling, pride for peace, and stepped boldly into the unknown, anchored in trust.

As you move through this book, let Pocahontas serve as a thread of inspiration, showing you that strength comes from surrender, not striving. Your identity is not something to earn, it's something to uncover. You were crowned for a reason, and this is the season to walk in it.

Gemstone Crown Progress Chart

Ruby – Courage

"Christ now gives us courage and confidence, so we can come to God by faith."
Ephesians 3:12 (CEV)

Sapphire – Wisdom

"...to give you spiritual wisdom and insight..."
Ephesians 1:17 (NLT)

Amethyst – Faith

"For it is by grace you have been saved, through faith..."
Ephesians 2:8

Emerald – Strength

"Strengthen you with power through his Spirit..."
Ephesians 3:16

Rose Quartz – Compassion

"Be kind and compassionate to one another, forgiving each other, just as in Christ God forgave you."
Ephesians 4:32

ONCE UPON A TIME...

Welcome.

You are here on purpose, for a purpose. God has a calling on your life. You were created and equipped for the good works He planned in advance for you to do. (Ephesians 2:10)

Warrior Princess, if only you could see yourself through God's eyes. He sees you as pure, righteous, and beautiful.

I remember the first time He spoke those words over me. I couldn't receive them. They felt so far from the broken pieces I saw in the mirror.

But little did I know, it wasn't me that was broken. It was the mirror. Shattered by pain, distorted by lies, and cracked by the past. When God held up the mirror of His love, I struggled to believe what I saw.

But that moment marked the beginning of my healing. And this, right here, this is the beginning of yours.

You're being drawn into God's truth spoken over you. He wants to heal your heart, transform your life, renew your mind, and equip your future.

Together, we'll walk through five core virtues found in the book of Ephesians: Courage, Wisdom, Faith, Strength, and Compassion.

Ephesians 2:10 NLT reminds us again:

"For we are God's masterpiece. He has created us anew in Christ Jesus, so we can do the good things he planned for us long ago."

Warrior Princess, take my hand as we begin.

I will walk with you through parts of my own story, the pain God has redeemed, the identity He restored, and the purpose He revealed. And the struggle that remains as we walk out our identity in Christ.

This is why we were created: to glorify God in all we think, say, and do.

God loves you so much that He sent His only Son, Jesus Christ, to die on the cross for your sins. It is a free gift, but one you must choose to receive.

And when you do, it changes everything.

Just like Cinderella, you are lifted from rags to royalty, a child of the Most High King, adopted into His royal family forever.

You are clothed in righteousness, crowned with authority, and filled with His Spirit to lead and guide you.

You are equipped with the full armor of God:

The sword of the Spirit

The shield of faith

The helmet of salvation

The breastplate of righteousness

And feet fitted with the gospel of peace

Stand your ground, putting on the belt of truth.

And pray in the Spirit on all occasions with all kinds of prayers and requests.

So look again into His mirror of truth: You are Pure. Righteous. Beautiful. He created you for the good works He planned just for you. You'll find the courage to step into what He's calling you to do. Wisdom is always available, just ask for it in every situation. And you'll walk by faith, believing in who you are in Him.

You will be strengthened by surrender, not striving. And love will overflow into compassion.

These five gems, Courage, Wisdom, Faith, Strength, and Compassion, will be set in your crown of gold.

A crown that represents His love.

A crown you will one day lay at His feet when your work is done.

Session 1:

Crowned for Courage

—

Ruby

Path to His Workmanship: My Courage Story

Crowned for Courage – Ruby

Scripture Focus

"Christ now gives us courage and confidence, so we can come to God by faith." (Ephesians 3:12, CEV)

Opening Reflection

Courage isn't the absence of fear. It's rising despite it. To be crowned with courage is to stand firm in the face of uncertainty, to speak truth even when your voice shakes, and to move forward when the path is unclear, because you trust the One who goes before you.

Live the Lesson

Consider this Challenge:

Do one thing this week that scares you but aligns with God's calling on your life.

Then reflect on what shifted within you when you did it.

Courage – The Path of His Workmanship

I didn't always feel courageous.

I knew how to look strong, but inside, I wrestled with fear, especially when God asked me to step into the unknown.

One of the most defining moments was when He asked me to surrender my daughter, not in the literal sense, but in trust. Like Abraham placing Isaac on the altar, I was called to lay her future in His hands. I had spent years trying to protect her, fix what I couldn't control, and carry the weight of outcomes that were never mine to hold. And then He whispered:

"Do you trust Me with what matters most to you?"

It didn't feel like courage at first. It felt like heartbreak.

But in the breaking, something holy formed: dependence. I began to see courage not as bold leaps, but as quiet obedience. Sometimes courage is just standing still and letting God fight for you. Sometimes it's saying yes when fear says no.

That surrender opened doors I never imagined: ministries, healing, and the discovery that my own identity wasn't in what I could control, but in what I was willing to release.

Courage, for me, is still unfolding.

But every time I say yes to Him, trembling or not, I see more clearly: I am His workmanship, and He's not done yet.

He is forming courage in me, one act of obedience at a time.

Pocahontas

A True Story of Courage

In 1608, Pocahontas risked her life to save Captain John Smith, stepping in front of him to stop her father's warriors. Later, during fragile peace talks, she was captured, baptized, and given the name Rebecca. Despite the hardship and hatred, she chose to live with dignity and faith. Eventually, she traveled to England as a cultural ambassador and a Christian convert. Her journey required courage not just to act, but to forgive and adapt, believing in a purpose far greater than her pain.

Biblical Parallel
Esther – The Hidden Queen with Bold Purpose

Courage – Esther

Courage

Esther was a Jewish orphan raised by her cousin Mordecai and eventually became queen of Persia. Though her beauty gained her favor, it was her bold faith that saved her people. When the Jews faced extermination, Esther risked her life by approaching King Xerxes uninvited. A crime punishable by death. Her famous words still echo: "If I perish, I perish."

Like Esther, Pocahontas stepped into unknown territory for the sake of others. Esther risked her life to approach the king to save her people. Both young women, full of courage, made bold moves that changed history. Esther's words, *"for such a time as this,"* remain relevant for ages.

Esther 4:14

Warrior Princess Profile

Discussion Prompts

THINK:

What does courage look like in your life right now?

_____

_____

_____

SAY:

Have you ever stood between two worlds like Pocahontas or Esther?

_____

_____

_____

DO:

How is God calling you to rise in courage personally, spiritually, or relationally?

_____

_____

_____

Reflection Journal

Deep Dive in the Word

Anchor Verse:

"Christ now gives us courage and confidence, so we can come to God by faith." (Ephesians 3:12, CEV)

Hebrew Word: amats – אָמַץ : to be strong, courageous, brave, alert

"Amats is like putting on your courage-armour and going for it…"

Hebrewwordlessons.com

Greek Word: tharseō – θαρσέω: to take heart, be courageous, bold, confident

tharseō in Ephesians 3:12 signifies the confident assurance and fearless access available to God's presence as a result of faith in Jesus Christ. (Strong's Greek: 2293)

Cross-References on Courage:

- Genesis 25:23- …"Two nations are in your womb…the one shall be stronger (amats) than the other…"
- Joshua 1:9 – "…Be strong and courageous. Do not be afraid… the Lord your God will be with you…."
- John 16:33 – "…In this world you will have trouble. But take heart (tharseō), I have overcome the world"

Reflection Questions

1. What's the difference between God-given courage and boldness rooted in pride?

   _____

   _____

   _____

2. Which courage verse resonated with you most today? Why?

   _____

   _____

   _____

3. What would it look like to walk in courage and your God-given identity this week?

   _____

   _____

   _____

Daily Armor: Belt of Truth (Ruby – Courage)

Spiritual Connection: Courage requires honesty with yourself, with others, and with God. The Belt of Truth gives you the confidence to stand firm, speak boldly, and walk in integrity, even when it's hard.

Key Verse: "Stand firm then, with the belt of truth buckled around your waist..." (Ephesians 6:14)

Prayer Focus:

"Lord, teach me how to be Your Warrior Princess and stand in courage. Fasten Your truth around my life today. Give me the boldness to walk in integrity and to speak with conviction, even when it costs me. Let Your truth be the belt that holds me steady so I can walk in courage and glorify You in all I think, say, and do."

Affirmation

I am courageous, not because I feel strong, but because God's strength is alive in me.

Session 2:

Crowned for Wisdom

–

Sapphire

Path to His Workmanship: My Wisdom Story

Crowned for Wisdom – Sapphire

Scripture Focus

"I pray that the eyes of your heart may be enlightened in order that you may know the hope to which He has called you, the riches of His glorious inheritance in His holy people." (Ephesians 1:18)

Opening Reflection

Wisdom is more than knowledge. It's discernment, understanding, and clarity that come from God. To walk in wisdom is to see with spiritual eyes, to make decisions led by truth, and to respond to life with insight and peace. Wisdom keeps us steady when emotions rise and circumstances shift. It is a crown of calm confidence and clarity.

Live the Lesson

Consider this challenge:

Slow down and seek God's perspective before making your next big decision.

Then, reflect on how inviting Him in changed the outcome of your peace.

Wisdom – The Path of His Workmanship

I've made decisions before that felt right at the time. They were based on what I could see, understand, or handle. Not because I was following others, but because I was relying on my own strength.

My own logic.

My survival instinct.

Over time, I've learned that wisdom isn't found in self-reliance. It's found in surrender.

It's found in His Word and in obedience.

At some point, I mistook independence for strength. I didn't want to be codependent, constantly looking to others for my worth or direction. But in my resistance, I ended up leaning into emotional independence. I shut people out and kept everything to myself.

But God didn't create me for either of those extremes. He created me for interdependence; rooted in Him, connected to others, and honest about my need for grace, guidance, and community.

Now, I listen differently.

I ask.

I wait.

I follow. Not perfectly, but with more humility than before.

He's still enlightening the eyes of my heart.

He's still shaping wisdom in me.

Pocahontas

A True Story of Wisdom

In a time of rising tension between the Jamestown settlers and the Powhatan people, Pocahontas was often the voice of calm and reason. She visited the settlement with food during famines, navigated relationships between two cultures, and eventually chose to walk a new path of faith and identity. Her wisdom showed in her restraint, her timing, and her ability to understand a bigger picture than those around her.

Biblical Parallel
Abigail – The Wise Intercessor and Warrior of Peace

Wisdom – Abigail

Wisdom

Abigail was the intelligent and discerning wife of Nabal, a foolish and harsh man. When David was prepared to destroy her household in anger, Abigail intervened with humility, wisdom, and courage. Her bold act of peacemaking averted bloodshed and won David's respect.

Like Abigail in 1 Samuel 25, Pocahontas used discernment to intervene in a moment of potential destruction. Abigail approached David with humility and wisdom, preventing bloodshed and preserving peace. Wisdom is often quiet but powerful.

> "...the wisdom that comes from heaven is first of all pure; then peace-loving, considerate, submissive, full of mercy and good fruit..." (James 3:17)

1 Samuel 25:32-33

Warrior Princess Profile

Discussion Prompts

THINK: How does spiritual wisdom shape your life?

_____

_____

_____

Reflect on how God's wisdom influences your thoughts, decisions, and priorities.

SAY: Can you think of a time when God gave you wisdom to speak into a situation?

What did you say, and how did it bring peace, clarity, or truth?

_____

_____

_____

DO: Is there a decision or relationship where wise action is needed right now?

How can you live out the wisdom God has given you this week?

_____

_____

_____

Reflection Journal

Deep Dive in the Word

Ephesians Anchor Verse:
"I pray that the eyes of your heart may be enlightened..." Ephesians 1:18a
(Greek: photizō – to illuminate, bring to light)

Hebrew Word: chokmah – חָכְמָה: wisdom, skill, insight, applied
knowledge. (Strong's Concordance H2451)

Greek Word: Sophia – σοφία: divine insight, clarity, prudence, full of
intelligence and spiritual understanding (Strong's Concordance G4678)

Cross-References:
- Exodus 28:3: Tell all the skilled workers to whom I have given wisdom
  in such matters that they are to make garments for Aaron, for his
  consecration, so he may serve me as priest."
  This verse specifically mentions the "wise-hearted" individuals who are
  filled with the "spirit of wisdom" to create Aaron's garments.
- Proverbs 4:7 (KJV) – "Wisdom is the principal thing; therefore get
  wisdom...."
- Colossians 1:9 – "...ask God to fill you with the knowledge of his will
  through all the wisdom and understanding that the Spirit gives."

Reflection Questions

1. How does the world's version of wisdom differ from God's?

_____

_____

_____

2. What does it mean to have "the eyes of your heart enlightened"?

_____

_____

_____

3. Where are you currently needing divine wisdom?

_____

_____

_____

Daily Armor: Helmet of Salvation (Sapphire - Wisdom)

Spiritual Connection: Wisdom begins with knowing who you are in Christ. The Helmet of Salvation guards your thoughts and helps you see with heavenly perspective, protecting your mind from confusion, fear, and lies.

Key Verse: "Take the helmet of salvation..." (Ephesians 6:17a)

Prayer Focus: Lord, cover my mind today with the helmet of salvation. Let Your truth guard my thoughts and give me wisdom to see clearly and think rightly. Keep me rooted in who You say I am that I may glorify You in all I think, say, and do.

Affirmation

I walk in wisdom, because God has opened the eyes of my heart and leads me with truth and clarity.

Session 3:

Crowned for Faith

—

Amethyst

Path to His Workmanship: My Faith Story

Crowned for Faith – Amethyst

Scripture Focus

"For it is by grace you have been saved, through faith - and this is not from yourselves, it is the gift of God - not by works, so that no one can boast." (Ephesians 2:8-9)

Opening Reflection

Faith is the doorway to everything God has for us. It's not about having all the answers. It's about trusting the One who does. Faith chooses to believe before it sees, to walk when the path is unclear, and to depend on grace rather than striving. To be crowned with faith is to anchor your identity in Christ and build your life on His promises, even when the world shakes.

Live the Lesson

Consider this Challenge:

Take a faith step in an area where fear or hesitation has held you back.

Whether it's a conversation, a decision, or an act of surrender, do it by faith.

Faith – The Path of His Workmanship

I've walked through storms that left me speechless.

Abuse.

Unplanned pregnancies.

Searching for love, for truth, for healing in all the wrong places, hoping something would fill the ache.

There were seasons when I was angry at God.

Not because I didn't believe He was real, but because I knew He was sovereign. And I couldn't understand why He allowed certain things to happen.

But even in my anger, I still clung to a quiet, desperate faith: He had a plan.

Even when I couldn't see it.

Even when I didn't want to hear it.

My faith in His sovereignty didn't erase my pain, but it anchored me in it.

It gave me the strength to cry out to Him, not just about Him.

Over time, I began to see that He wasn't absent. He was weaving purpose through the wreckage.

Now, when I look back, I don't just see broken pieces. I see grace woven through every part.

He met me in the aftermath, healed what I thought was beyond repair, and began writing something beautiful with the pieces I had surrendered.

For me, faith isn't about having all the answers. It's about choosing to believe that He is good, even when life hasn't been.

It's about knowing I am His workmanship, even when I feel undone.

He is still anchoring my faith. He's still writing my redemption.

And I am still saying yes.

Pocahontas
A True Story of Faith

Pocahontas didn't just adapt to a new culture; she embraced a new identity in Christ. Baptized as Rebecca, she stepped into a life of faith despite all she had endured. Her willingness to walk forward into the unknown, to leave behind what was familiar, and to believe in something greater than herself, was a testimony of quiet, unshakable faith. Her story reminds us that faith sometimes looks like surrender and other times like courage.

Biblical Parallel
Mary Magdalene – The Devoted Witness of Resurrection

Faith – Mary Magdalene

Faith

Mary Magdalene was healed by Jesus, who cast out seven demons from her (Luke 8:2). After that, she became one of His most faithful followers. She not only supported His ministry but also stood by Him at the cross when others fled. And when He rose from the dead, it was Mary who was the first to see Him and share the good news.

Like Mary Magdalene, Pocahontas experienced identity transformation through faith. Both women left behind old reputations to walk in their divine calling. Their lives testify that true faith is not about having all the answers, but about surrendering to the One who does.

Luke 8:2, John 20:16-18

Warrior Princess Profile

Discussion Prompts

THINK: What does "faith as a gift" mean to you personally?

_____

_____

_____

SAY: What has tested your faith in the past, and how did God show up?

_____

_____

_____

DO: Where is He calling you to trust Him more fully now?
(Write a prayer asking God to grow your faith and guide your steps.)

_____

_____

_____

Reflection Journal

_____
_____
_____
_____
_____
_____
_____
_____
_____
_____
_____
_____
_____
_____
_____
_____
_____
_____
_____
_____
_____
_____
_____
_____
_____
_____
_____
_____
_____

Deep Dive in the Word

Ephesians Anchor Verse:

"For it is by grace you have been saved, through faith..." (Ephesians 2:8–9)

Hebrew Word: emunah – אֱמוּנָה : steadfastness, trust, faithfulness, firmness. (Strong's Concordance H530)

Greek Word: pistis – πίστις: faith as trust, loyalty, and confidence in God's promises (Strong's Greek: 4102)

Cross-References:

- Hebrews 11:6 – "Without faith it is impossible to please God..."
- 2 Corinthians 5:7 – "For we live by faith, not by sight."
- Romans 10:17 – So then faith *comes* by hearing, and hearing by the word of God. (NKJV)"

Reflection Questions

1. When has faith felt risky for you but proven worth it?

   _____

   _____

   _____

2. How does grace change the way you live out your faith?

   _____

   _____

   _____

3. What's one area you need to place fully in God's hands?

   _____

   _____

   _____

Daily Armor: Shield of Faith (Amethyst – Faith)

Armor Piece: Shield

Spiritual Connection: Faith is your protection when the enemy attacks. The Shield of Faith guards you from fear, doubt, and discouragement, extinguishing lies with the truth of God's promises.

Key Verse: "...Take up the shield of faith, with which you can extinguish all the flaming arrows of the evil one." (Ephesians 6:16)

Prayer Focus:

Lord, help me reflect You as a Warrior Princess today. Be my Shield of Faith and my Strength. Fortify my heart so I can stand firm against every lie and fiery dart of the enemy. Let my life be marked by bold trust, unwavering confidence, and quiet courage, even before I see the victory. May everything I think, say, and do bring glory to You.

Affirmation

I walk by faith, not by sight, because my life is built on His grace, not my striving.

Session 4:

Crowned for Strength

–

Emerald

Path to His Workmanship: My Strength Story

Crowned for Strength - Emerald

Scripture Focus

"I pray that out of his glorious riches he may strengthen you with power through his Spirit in your inner being." (Ephesians 3:16)

Opening Reflection

True strength is not loud or forceful; it's steady, enduring, and anchored in Christ. To be crowned for strength means you stand when others fall, you carry burdens with grace, and you draw your power from a source deeper than yourself. God's strength is perfected in our weakness, giving us the ability to persevere with purpose.

Live the Lesson

Spend time in prayer asking God to strengthen you, not just physically or emotionally, but spiritually and internally.

Then, reflect on how His strength sustains you differently than your effort.

Consider this challenge:

Think of a situation where you've been trying to carry the weight alone, whether emotionally, physically, or mentally. What would it look like to surrender that burden to God and ask for His supernatural strength instead?

Strength – The Path to His Workmanship

Strength wasn't something I asked for. It's just something life demanded of me.

There were days I didn't feel strong at all. But I couldn't afford to fall apart, so I pushed through. I carried the weight, made things work, and I called that strength.

But it wasn't until I left my family, friends, and church to become a traveling therapist, totally dependent on God, that I began to understand true strength.

He met me in my pain.
Still, it wasn't until I ran out.
Out of energy.
Out of answers.
Out of myself.
I finally realized that real strength doesn't come from within me.

It comes from within Him.

God doesn't just give us the strength to survive the battle
He becomes our strength in the middle of it. He met me when I was worn out, poured out, and flat on my face. He didn't tell me to toughen up. He whispered, "Come to Me."

And in His presence, I found a strength that didn't rely on my effort
Only on my surrender.

I'm learning now that being strong doesn't always look like standing tall.
Sometimes it looks like kneeling.
Sometimes it looks like asking for help.
Sometimes it looks like resting in the arms of the One who never runs out of power.

He is still strengthening me in the deepest parts of who I am.
And it's in that hidden place...
I stand.

Pocahontas
A True Story of Strength

During her captivity at Jamestown, Pocahontas was separated from her family, her culture, and the life she had known. Yet during this time, she grew in grace and inner resilience. She learned the language and faith of her captors and chose to forgive. Rather than resist out of fear or revenge, she embodied quiet strength, one that chose healing over hatred. Her inner resolve carried her into a new identity, a new name, and eventually, a new purpose.

Biblical Parallel
Ruth – The Loyal Redeemed Sojourner

Strength – Ruth

Strength

Ruth, a Moabite widow, chose loyalty over comfort. After her husband died, she clung to her mother-in-law Naomi, declaring, "Your people will be my people, and your God my God." Her faith and humility led her to Boaz, her kinsman redeemer, and she became the great-grandmother of King David.

Like Ruth, Pocahontas walked away from what was familiar and stepped into a new land, trusting in a greater purpose. Both women showed strength through loyalty, humility, and unwavering resolve. Their stories reveal that strength is often quiet and rooted in love.

Ruth 1:16-17

Warrior Princess Profile

Discussion Prompts

THINK: Where does true strength come from, and how is it different from self-reliance?

_____

_____

_____

SAY: What declaration reminds me that God's power is made perfect in my weakness?

_____

_____

_____

DO: What can I do today that requires me to lean on God's strength, not my own?

_____

_____

_____

Reflection Journal

_____
_____
_____
_____
_____
_____
_____
_____
_____
_____
_____
_____
_____
_____
_____
_____
_____
_____
_____
_____
_____
_____
_____
_____
_____
_____
_____
_____
_____
_____

Deep Dive in the Word

Hebrew Word: chazaq – חָזַק: to strengthen, prevail, become mighty, be courageous (Strong's Concordance H2388)

Greek Word: krataioō – κραταιόω: to be empowered, become strong inwardly (Strong's Concordance G2901)

Ephesians Anchor Verse:

"...I pray that out of his glorious riches he may strengthen you with power through his Spirit in your inner being," (Ephesians 3:16)

(Greek: krataioō – strength that builds within, fortified by the Spirit)

Cross-References:

- Isaiah 40:29 – "He gives strength to the weary and increases the power of the weak."
- 2 Corinthians 12:9 – "...My power is made perfect in weakness."
- Philippians 4:13 (NKJV) – "I can do all things through Christ who strengthens me."

Reflection Questions

1. Where do you currently draw your strength from, and how has that source shaped your identity?

   _____

   _____

   _____

2. Can you recall a time when God's strength carried you through a situation you felt too weak to handle? What did you learn about Him and yourself?

   _____

   _____

   _____

3. What lies have you believed about being "strong"? (e.g., "I have to do everything alone," "Crying is weakness") What truth from God's Word can replace those lies?

   _____

   _____

   _____

Daily Armor: Breastplate of Righteousness (Emerald – Strength)

Spiritual Connection: Strength comes from living in the right standing with God. The Breastplate of Righteousness protects your heart, guarding your identity and integrity, so you can stand firm and endure with holy confidence.

Key Verse: "...with the breastplate of righteousness in place..." (Ephesians 6:14)

Prayer Focus

Lord, I am Your daughter, a Warrior Princess. Because of You, I am strong.

Protect my heart today with Your righteousness.

Help me walk uprightly, live with integrity, and stand firm in the identity You've given me.

Let Your righteousness be my defense and covering in every thought, word, and action.

Affirmation

I am strong, not because I have it all together, but because the Spirit of God is alive and working in me.

Session 5:

Crowned for Compassion

–

Rose Quartz

Path to His Workmanship: My Compassion Story

Crowned for Compassion – Rose Quartz

Scripture Focus

"Be kind and compassionate to one another, forgiving each other, just as in Christ God forgave you." Ephesians 4:32

Opening Reflection

Compassion is the strength of a tender heart. It's the ability to feel deeply, and to act in love. True compassion doesn't look away from pain; it leans in with grace, mercy, and empathy. To be crowned with compassion is to reflect the heart of Christ, to see the broken, love the hurting, and forgive the undeserving, just as He did for us.

Live the Lesson

Reach out to someone who needs kindness. Offer empathy, not answers.

Let the act of compassion soften your heart and strengthen your spirit.

Consider this challenge:

Think of someone who may be carrying silent pain. What would it look like to lead with compassion instead of assumptions?

Compassion doesn't wait until it's convenient. It sees the need and responds.

Compassion – The Path of His Workmanship

Compassion didn't come easily for me, not in the way God was calling me to live it.

I knew how to show up strong, how to take care of things. But the kind of compassion that slows down, forgives deeply, and softens hard places? That took a loss.

When my sister died, everything changed.

Suddenly, life felt too short to hold grudges, too precious to waste in pride, pain, or regret. That's when God started whispering to me:

"Live with nothing left unsaid. Forgive the unforgivable. Remember what I sacrificed for you."

Her death cracked something open in me. It made space for grace. For compassion that doesn't wait for an apology. For love that covers even the sharp edges.

And it reminded me: Jesus didn't wait for me to deserve compassion; He gave it freely.

So who am I to withhold it?

I don't always get it right. I still wrestle with boundaries and trust, and giving second chances. But I'm learning to live softer. To forgive quicker. To see people through His eyes, not just mine.

He is still shaping compassion in me. And every time I choose love instead of fear, grace instead of bitterness, I know I'm growing more like Him.

Pocahontas: A True Story of Compassion

Pocahontas is remembered not only for her courage, but also for her deep compassion, a love that moved her to action even in the face of danger and division.

When tensions rose between her people and the English settlers, Pocahontas often served as a peacemaker. She risked her safety to bring food and aid to the colonists during a time of famine, showing kindness to those who might have been seen as enemies. Most famously, she intervened to save the life of John Smith, an act not just of bravery, but of profound compassion. She saw past fear and hostility and chose mercy.

Though she was young, Pocahontas understood something powerful: Compassion bridges gaps that fear cannot. She valued life, peace, and unity, even when it cost her personally.

Biblical Parallel

The Samaritan Woman – The Redeemed Witness at the Well

Compassion – The Samaritan Woman

Compassion:

She came to the well alone at midday, when no one else would be there. This woman had a past. Five husbands. One live-in partner. And a reputation that made her an outcast. But Jesus didn't avoid her. He went out of His way to find her. He revealed her sin, then offered her living water. Transformed by grace, she became one of the first evangelists, telling her village, "Come, see a man who told me everything I ever did!"

In many ways, the Samaritan Woman (John 4) was like Pocahontas, someone others never expected to carry compassion or purpose. Yet after her encounter with Jesus, everything changed. She didn't wait for approval or permission. Instead, she rushed back to the very people who had once shamed her, bringing them to Christ. Her compassion didn't wait for the approval. It flowed from the grace she had received.

John 4:28-30,39

Warrior Princess Profile

Discussion Prompts

THINK: How is compassion different from pity or guilt?

_____

_____

_____

SAY: Who is God asking you to see through His eyes today?

_____

_____

_____

DO: What specific act of compassion can I offer this week, especially to someone overlooked?

_____

_____

_____

Reflection Journal

_____
_____
_____
_____
_____
_____
_____
_____
_____
_____
_____
_____
_____
_____
_____
_____
_____
_____
_____
_____
_____
_____
_____
_____
_____
_____
_____
_____

Deep Dive in the Word

Hebrew Word: chazaq – חָזַק: to strengthen, prevail, become mighty, be courageous (Strong's Concordance H2388)

Greek Word: krataioō – κραταιόω: to be empowered, become strong inwardly (Strong's Concordance G2901)

Ephesians Anchor Verse:

"...I pray that out of his glorious riches he may strengthen you with power through his Spirit in your inner being," (Ephesians 3:16)

(Greek: krataioō – strength that builds within, fortified by the Spirit)

Cross-References:

- Isaiah 40:29 – "He gives strength to the weary and increases the power of the weak."
- 2 Corinthians 12:9 – "...My power is made perfect in weakness."
- Philippians 4:13 (NKJV) – "I can do all things through Christ who strengthens me."

Reflection Questions

1. Where do you currently draw your strength from, and how has that source shaped your identity?

_____

_____

_____

2. Can you recall a time when God's strength carried you through a situation you felt too weak to handle? What did you learn about Him and yourself?

_____

_____

_____

3. What lies have you believed about being "strong"? (e.g., "I have to do everything alone," "Crying is weakness") What truth from God's Word can replace those lies?

_____

_____

_____

Daily Armor: Shoes of Peace (Rose Quartz -Compassion)

Spiritual Connection: Compassion means carrying peace into pain. This peace comes from knowing the Good News, that Jesus died and rose again to restore us to right relationship with God. The Shoes of Peace equip you to step into broken spaces with calm, courage, and kindness, bringing the presence of Christ where others might retreat. His peace goes before you, steadies your spirit, and anchors your love in action.

Key Verse: "…and with your feet fitted with the readiness that comes from the gospel of peace." Ephesians 6:15 (NIV)

These are the Shoes of Peace, preparing you to walk in compassion and carry the Gospel wherever you go.

Prayer focus: Lord, You have crowned me with compassion and called me to walk toward the hurting, not away. Help me stand in peace, not panic. Let me move with purpose in all I think, say, and do, wearing the Shoes of Peace You've given me.

Affirmation

I am compassionate because the peace of my salvation moves me to step out in obedience and reach the hurting.

Session 6:

Crowned for Love

–

Gold

Path to His Workmanship: My Love Story

Crowned for Love – Gold

Scripture Focus

"...And I pray that you, being rooted and established in love, may have power... to grasp how wide and long and high and deep is the love of Christ." Ephesians 3:17–18

Opening Reflection

Love is your foundation. It's what roots you, strengthens you, and sets you apart. As a Warrior Princess, love is not just a feeling. It's your lifeline, your anchor, and your calling.

Live the Lesson

Consider this Challenge:

Where in your life is God inviting you to go deeper in love, wider in grace, stronger in forgiveness, or bolder in compassion?

_____
_____
_____

Love– The Path of His Workmanship

"We are God's handiwork , created in Christ Jesus to do good works, which God prepared in advance for us to do." (Ephesians 2:10)

Gold has always represented value. Beauty. Glory.
But in the Kingdom of God, gold means something deeper. It means love. It means purpose. It's the thread that holds every gem in place. The power behind every act of obedience. The legacy that outlasts our circumstances.

For a long time, I wondered what my life would amount to.
I carried wounds, mistakes, and shame that felt like disqualifiers.
But God didn't see a ruined story. He saw His workmanship in process.

He began to show me that every moment I surrendered, He redeemed. Every part of my journey, the pain, the healing, the rebuilding, was shaping me into something that would reflect His light.

Gold is not about being perfect. It's about being refined. It's about being crowned not by what I've done, but by who He is in me.

Now, I don't just wear a crown, I carry a purpose.
To love.
To teach.
To forgive.
To speak life.
To walk in truth.
To equip other Warrior Princesses for the good works He prepared in advance.

One day, I'll lay my crown at His feet, not out of defeat, but because I've lived in the delight of fulfilling what He wrote for me. Every gem I've placed, every step I took in obedience, was for His glory.

This is the legacy I carry.
This is the love I was shaped by.
This is the gold that crowns me.

Pocahontas
A True Story of Love

When Pocahontas embraced a new name and identity as Rebecca Rolfe, it wasn't just a diplomatic alliance; it was an act of surrender and love. She let go of the comfort of familiarity, choosing to walk in peace and reconciliation between cultures that had once been at war.

Her decision to marry, to travel across the ocean, and to carry herself with grace in foreign lands wasn't rooted in obligation. It was rooted in a deep, sacrificial love. She bore misunderstandings and separated from her people so that peace could be achieved. She lived out a love that gave more than it received.

Her legacy is not just about courage or diplomacy; it's about choosing love when bitterness would have been justified.

She reminds us that love costs something...

But the fruit of love surrendered to God endures beyond generations.

Biblical Parallel
Hannah – The Faithful Intercessor and Mother of Promise

Love – Hannah

Love

Hannah's story begins in quiet anguish. Though deeply loved by her husband, Elkanah, she bore the shame of barrenness. Mocked and misunderstood, she brought her pain to God. She wept, worshiped, and made a vow: "If You give me a son, I will give him back to You." God honored her prayer, and she kept her vow. Samuel's birth became the foundation of prophetic leadership in Israel.

Like Hannah, Pocahontas gave something deeply personal as an offering of love and surrender. Hannah gave her son to God; Pocahontas gave up her familiar world to walk in a new faith. Both women embodied sacrificial love that bore fruit for generations.

1 Samuel 1:10-11, 27-28

Warrior Princess Profile

Discussion Prompts

THINK: What does it look like to fight with love instead of fear, bitterness, or control?

_____

_____

_____

SAY: Share a time when choosing love cost you something but reflected Christ.

_____

_____

_____

DO: How can we love others without compromising truth or enabling harm?

_____

_____

_____

Reflection Journal

Deep Dive in the Word

Courage: agapē (ἀγάπη) – Selfless, unconditional, divine love.

Key Cross-References:

- 1 Corinthians 13:13 – "...The greatest of these is love."
- John 15:12 – "My command is this: Love each other as I have loved you."
- 1 Peter 4:8 – "...Love covers over a multitude of sins."
- Romans 5:5 – "...God's love has been poured out into our hearts through the Holy Spirit..."

Reflection Questions

1. Where in your life is God inviting you to be rooted in love rather than driven by fear, pride, or offense?

   _____

   _____

   _____

2. What does it mean to be established in love, not just receiving it but radiating it?

   _____

   _____

   _____

3. How wide and deep is the love of Christ in your story right now?

   _____

   _____

   _____

Daily Armor: Sword of the Spirit & Prayer (Gold – Love)

Crowned in Gold – The Sword and Prayer

Gold represents love, the divine thread that holds every gem in place. But gold is also radiant, powerful, and holy. In the Armor of God, it reflects our two greatest spiritual weapons: the Sword of the Spirit and Prayer.

Sword of the Spirit

The Sword of the Spirit is the Word of God. It's not just for defense, it's for declaring truth and advancing in battle. Every Warrior Princess must learn to wield the Word. Speak it. Memorize it. Pray it. Live it. Your sword is sharp when your heart is surrendered.

"Take... the sword of the Spirit, which is the word of God." (Ephesians 6:17).

Prayer

Prayer is the power that activates the entire armor. It is communion with your Commander. It keeps you aligned with heaven and strengthens you from within. It is not a piece of armor. It is your battle strategy.

"And pray in the Spirit on all occasions with all kinds of prayers and requests...." (Ephesians 6:18).

Warrior Princess Prayer

Lord, I pick up my sword today: Your Word. Teach me how to use it with wisdom and authority. Let it be on my lips, in my heart, and ready for battle. And Father, clothe me in prayer. Let every breath be in step with You. Train me to pray without ceasing, to listen as much as I speak, and to war with love. Crown me in gold. Not for my glory, but so I may reflect Yours.

> "For our struggle is not against flesh and blood, but against the rulers, against the authorities, against the powers of this dark world and the spiritual forces of evil in the heavenly realms." (Ephesians 6:12).

This Is a Spiritual Battle

As Warrior Princesses, we must remember: the real enemy is not people. The battle is spiritual. The wounds are invisible. The strategies of darkness are subtle, but God has equipped us to stand firm.

When you feel misunderstood, overlooked, attacked, or overwhelmed, stop and remember:

- The person is not your enemy.
- The pressure is not the end.
- The pain is not without purpose.

You were given armor not just to survive, but to stand. To resist the enemy. To fight from victory, not for it.

Put on the armor. Lift your eyes. This is not just about today, it's about eternity.

Session 7:

Commissioned for Your Calling

Devotional: Jesus – Our Example in the Armor

Scripture Focus:

"Put on the full armor of God, so that you can take your stand against the devil's schemes." Ephesians 6:11.

Reflection Passage:

Read Matthew 4:1–11 and Ephesians 6:10–18

Before Jesus began His ministry, He was led into the wilderness to face Satan's temptations. In that spiritual battle, He didn't just resist. He demonstrated how to wear the Armor of God.

1. Belt of Truth
Temptation: "Turn these stones to bread…"
Jesus' Response: "It is written…"
Jesus stood firm in the truth of God's Word.

Reflection: Where do you need to fasten the belt of truth today?

_____

_____

_____

2. Breastplate of Righteousness
Temptation: To use power apart from God's will.
Jesus' Response: He remained obedient and sinless.
Jesus chose what was right, not what was easy.

Reflection: Is there an area where you need to guard your heart with righteousness?

_____

_____

_____

3. Shoes of the Gospel of Peace

Temptation: "Throw Yourself down..."
Jesus' Response: "Do not test the Lord your God."
He stood in peace, not pressure.

Reflection: Are you walking in peace or reacting in fear?

_____

_____

_____

4. Shield of Faith

Temptation: "Bow to me and I'll give you everything..."
Jesus' Response: "Worship the Lord your God and serve Him only."
Faith deflected the lie and trusted the Father's timing.

Reflection: What arrows of doubt do you need to block with faith?

_____

_____

_____

5. Helmet of Salvation

Temptation: "If You are the Son of God..."
Jesus' Response: He knew His identity and purpose.
The helmet guarded His mind and mission.

Reflection: What truth about who you are in Christ do you need to reclaim?

_____

_____

_____

6. Sword of the Spirit – The Word of God

Temptation: In every attack
Jesus' Response: "It is written..."
He didn't fight with opinion. He fought with Scripture.

Reflection: What Scripture can you memorize and declare in battle?

_____

_____

_____

Closing Prayer

Lord Jesus, thank You for showing me how to stand as Your Warrior Princess. When I face temptation, remind me that Your Word is my weapon and Your example is my strategy. Clothe me in Your armor. Help me resist not only sin, but also distraction and discouragement. Strengthen me to stand firm in truth, to fight with faith, and to walk in victory.

May I glorify You in all I think, say, and do.

Amen.

Session 8:

Armor to Assignment

–

The Great Commission

Devotional: From Armor to Assignment – Living the Great Commission

Commissioning – From Armor to Assignment
Theme: Commissioned for Your Calling. Prepared for His Purpose

Scripture Focus: "Go therefore and make disciples of all nations... and behold, I am with you always, to the end of the age." (Matthew 28:19–20, ESV)

From Wilderness to Witness
Jesus didn't just overcome temptation in the wilderness; He overcame sin, death, and the grave. After rising in victory, He gave His final command: Go. This wasn't a suggestion. It was a sending. He equips us with the Armor of God, and then He commissions us to walk in authority.

You are not just crowned for protection. You are crowned for a purpose.

• Belt of Truth: Walk in truth and speak it boldly.
• Breastplate of Righteousness: Live with integrity as a light in a dark world.
• Shoes of Peace: Bring the Gospel wherever you go.
• Shield of Faith: Keep trusting, even when the way is hard.
• Helmet of Salvation: Remember who you are and whose you are.
• Sword of the Spirit: Speak the Word to bring life and freedom.
You rise, not just to stand strong, but to go forth and shine.

Reflection Questions

1. Where is God calling you to "go"? (Home, work, ministry, mission field?)

_____

_____

_____

2. Which part of the armor do you need to strengthen before stepping out?

_____

_____

_____

3. How can you use your story to disciple others?

_____

_____

_____

Closing Declaration

I am crowned for purpose.

I wear His armor not just to stand, but to walk.

I carry His truth, His peace, His love, and His name.

I am commissioned to go, empowered to lead, and appointed to shine.

Final Declaration:
You Don't Just Stand in Armor,
You Walk in Authority

I am a Warrior Princess, Crowned for Purpose.

You Don't Just Stand in Armor, You Walk in Authority

I don't just wear the armor of God; I wield it with divine authority.

I was created, called, and commissioned by the King of Kings.

I walk boldly in truth, stand firm in righteousness, move forward in peace, and stand strong in faith.

I guard my heart with salvation and speak life with the sword of the Spirit.

I don't shrink back from battle.

I don't wait for permission.

I've been given authority through Christ to tear down strongholds, stand against the enemy, and walk in purpose with power.

My crown is not for comfort; it's a sign of my commission.

I've been prepared. I have been positioned.

Now I will walk not just as one who survives but as one who reigns through grace to glorify You in all I think, say, and do.

In Jesus' name,

Ephesians 4:1b NIV

"...I urge you to live a life worthy of the calling you have received."

Session 9:

The Crowning Ceremony

Commissioning Ceremony: Crowned for Purpose, Sent with Power

"Daughters of the King, Warrior Princesses crowned for purpose, you have been equipped with the armor of God and filled with the Spirit of truth. But armor is not for decoration. It's for deployment. Today, you are not only warriors, you are witnesses. You are not only protected, you are commissioned."

WARRIOR PRINCESS TRIBE COMMITMENT

As a member of the Warrior Princess Tribe,
I choose to walk in strength, grace, and purpose.

I commit to:

- **Embrace my identity** as a daughter of the King-royal by birth, refined by trials, and crowned with purpose.
- **Pursue a heart of courage**, rising in boldness when fear whispers lies.
- **Cultivate wisdom**, seeking truth through God's Word and listening for His voice
- **Stand in strength,** even in weakness, knowing the Lord is my Rock and Refuge.
- **Extend compassion** to myself and others, serving with tenderness and love.
- **Live by faith,** trusting God's plan even when the path is unclear.
- **Honor my sisters,** lifting them up with encouragement, truth, and accountability.
- **Protect the unity** of this tribe, standing together in love, not comparison.
- **Uphold integrity,** choosing character over comfort, obedience over ease.
- **Leave a legacy,** walking out my calling with honor, perseverance, and joy.

I am not alone. I am not forgotten. I am not powerless.

I am a WARRIOR PRINCESS
Crowned for Purpose.

Warrior Princess - His Workmanship

"...I pray that you, being rooted and established in love, may have power... to grasp how wide and long and high and deep is the love of Christ, and to know this love that surpasses knowledge." – (Ephesians 3:17-19).

Love is not always soft.

Sometimes it looks like a sacrifice.

For me, love meant giving deeply, painfully, and intentionally.

I placed not one, but three children for adoption. Each decision was born out of heartbreak and healing.

After surviving the trauma of date rape, I was angry-angry at the injustice, the shame, and the pain of it all. I didn't want my child growing up in an unhealthy, unstable environment. But I also knew I couldn't carry the weight alone.

Still, I was caught in a cycle, seeking comfort in the only way I knew how. I kept hoping it would fill the ache, but instead it repeated the pain. With each unexpected pregnancy came the crushing choice: would I hold on... or surrender in love?

There were times I considered the so-called "easy" way out.

But every time, God intervened.

Those decisions will always mark my life. But they are also monuments of grace.

Each child placed was an act of love deeper than words.

Each moment of surrender became a doorway to healing for them and for me.

And today, by God's mercy, I'm still connected to two of them.

Their stories continue, and so does mine, woven together by the love that let go.

God is still writing my story. Still redeeming broken places with His love. Still teaching me that when I give in love, I never truly lose.

ABOUT THE AUTHOR AND FOUNDER

Ann Marie Cooper is a trauma-informed life coach, Certified Trauma Healing Facilitator, and speaker. She is the founder of TRUE Trauma Healing, with a heart for restoration and a deep passion for purpose. Ann Marie seeks to inspire women to rise from brokenness and walk boldly in their God-given identity. Her journey through abuse, grief, single motherhood, and ministry has shaped her approach to life, bringing truth, authenticity, and hope into every space she enters.

As the creator of the *Warrior Princess: Crowned for Purpose* devotional and retreat, Ann Marie leads a faith-based ministry that helps women embrace the virtues of Courage, Wisdom, Faith, Strength, and Compassion. Whether she's leading retreats, mentoring women, or facilitating healing groups, her mission is clear: to remind every daughter of the King that she was created for more, on purpose, with purpose.

Ann Marie Cooper lives in North Carolina with her daughter, where she continues to champion healing, legacy, and kingdom identity in every season of life.

SPECIAL THANKS

A very special thanks to Agnes Stasik,
the owner of Ideal Moment Photography.

No words could describe how grateful and thankful I am for the wonderful job Agnes did on my cover and my author photo! Her creativity and expertise are just a small portion of the wonderful person the world is gifted to see. I couldn't have had this beautiful project without her, and because of that, I had to share her contact details with my readers. I know without a doubt that the results will touch your heart the way her work did mine.

Ideal Moment Photography
Serving Charlotte, NC to Lancaster County
Idealmomentphotography.com
1661 Walkup Ave Suite H
Monroe, NC 28110
(980) 327-6681

www.ingramcontent.com/pod-product-compliance
Lightning Source LLC
Chambersburg PA
CBHW072128090426
42739CB00012B/3108